The Rockwool Foundation Research Unit

Study Paper No. 99

Introduction to the project: Employment Effects of Entrepreneurs

Johan M. Kuhn, Nikolaj Malchow-Møller and Anders Sørensen

University Press of Southern Denmark

Odense 2015

Introduction to the project: Employment Effects of Entrepreneurs

Study Paper No. 99

Published by:
The Rockwool Foundation research Unit and
University press of Southern Denmark

Address:
The Rockwool Foundation Research Unit
Soelvgade 10, 2.tv.
DK-1307 Copenhagen K

Telephone   +45 33 34 48 00
E-mail   forskningsenheden@rff.dk
web site: www.en.rff.dk

ISBN 978-87-93119-26-0
ISSN 0908-3979

November 2015

Introduction to the project:

Employment Effects of Entrepreneurs

Johan M. Kuhn, Department of International Economics and Management, Copenhagen Business School, Porcelænshaven 16A, DK-2000 Frederiksberg, Denmark (tel: +45 3815 3467, email: jmk.int@cbs.dk)

*Nikolaj Malchow-Møller, Department of Business and Economics, University of Southern Denmark, Campusvej 55, 5230 Odense M, Danmark (tel: **+45** 6550 2109, email: nmm@sam.sdu.dk)*

Anders Sørensen (corresponding author), Department of Economics, Copenhagen Business School, Porcelænshaven 16 Porcelænshaven 16A, DK-2000 Frederiksberg, Denmark (tel: +45 3815 3493, email: as.eco@cbs.dk).

Abstract:

In this note a short introduction to the project "Employment Effects of Entrepreneurs" is presented. First, we describe the purpose of the project; second, we present the background; third, we briefly describe the three papers that constitute the output of the project, and fourth, we discuss two important qualifications for the understanding of the contributions and results established in the project.

Acknowledgements: We are greatly indebted to the *Rockwool Foundation* for funding of this project, and Statistics Denmark for providing the data.

1. Purpose

In the project "Employment Effects of Entrepreneurs" we study two aspects of jobs in start-ups and incumbent firms. The first aspect is *job creation*. Specifically, we investigate the importance of start-ups and incumbent firms, respectively, for job creation in the Danish economy. The main purpose is to develop a new framework for measuring job creation and destruction by different types of firms; a new framework that distinguishes between different firm types and different job types, and which takes the potential simultaneity in the creation and destruction of jobs across firms into account. Specifically, we distinguish between the educational content of jobs. The applied definition of an entrepreneurial firm in this project is the organic start-up (or nascent firm) and not justthe formally new firms. The exact definition of the organic start-up is described below in Section 4.

The second aspect that we study is the characteristics of jobs in start-ups compared to those of jobs in incumbent firms. Even though this question has been addressed by many researchers before us, we provide new evidence to the field because we are able to identify the organic new firms. As our main purpose is to characterize jobs and to compare them across firm types, we base the analysis on the following dependent variables: wages, skill intensities, labour productivity and total factor productivity (TFP). The latter measure is not a job-specific measure. However, it is partly based on firms' labour inputs and therefore indirectly includes important information about job characteristics. We also distinguishing between firms located in growing industry-region clusters and firms located in declining industry-region clusters. The motivation for this is to study whether the business environment of the firms is important for the job characteristics.

Finally, we consider the characteristics of jobs in spinoff firms and compare them to jobs in non-spinoff entrepreneurial firms. If spinoffs play an important role as an engine for growth and prosperity (which is often considered to be the case), we would expect jobs created by these firms to be of higher quality than jobs created in other entrepreneurial firms. As described above, we also distinguish between firms located in growing industry-region clusters and firms located in declining industry-region clusters.

2. Background

In this section we briefly describe the existing literature of relevance for the topics that we address in the project. For specific references to contributions in the literature, we refer the reader to the descriptions and reference lists of the individual papers of the project.

The empirical testing of job creation by entrepreneurs on actual job data started back in the 1980's, when Birch (1981, 1987) claimed that small firms (many of which are young as well) were the main driver of US job creation. Birch (1987) found that firms with fewer than 20 employees accounted for 88 percent of overall employment growth in the USA between 1981 and 1985. In the wake of Birch's initial analyses, a large number of studies have analysed the role of small and new firms in the job-creation process using data on firm- or establishment-level worker flows. Most of these studies rely on the methodology developed in Davis and Haltiwanger (1992) and Davis et al. (1996), where measures of job creation and job destruction are defined.

The general message to emerge from this literature is that small firms (or establishments) tend to contribute more to both gross and net job creation than larger firms (or establishments). But although start-ups are typically small, and small firms are often young, the two sets of firms are not identical. However, the number of studies that have looked at the role of new establishments or new firms in the job-creation process is more limited and only few studies distinguish new establishments belonging to new firms from new establishments belonging to old firms. Still, the general result from this literature is that new establishments or new firms contribute significantly more to gross and net job creation then older establishments/firms.

Most of the studies in the literature do not distinguish between different types of jobs, and those that do so are disaggregating by employer characteristics like industry. None of the studies distinguish between different types of jobs created (and destroyed) within a firm, probably due to a lack of data. Therefore, an important contribution of this project to distinguish between different job types (using educational attainment of the job holder) in job creation and destruction.

Next, we turn to the literature on job quality in entrepreneurial firms. Entrepreneurs are often considered to play an important role as an engine for growth and prosperity. In the words of Schumpeter (1934, 1943), entrepreneurs create combinations of inputs and outputs to pioneer new activities, exploit new market opportunities and allocate labour to its most productive use. However, entrepreneurship is not always found to be good business for those involved in entrepreneurial projects.

The majority of studies in the economic literature have found that entrepreneurs pay lower wages than other firms and hire employees with lower levels of human capital. Moreover, the productivity levels and income of entrepreneurs are found to be of similar magnitude or lower than in established firms.

As for the studies of job creation, the studies of job characteristics in entrepreneurship use a definition of entrepreneurial firms that are based on establishment/firm size or age. These studies find that small or younger firms pay lower wages. It is also found that older firms pay higher wages, but once you control for worker characteristics the difference disappears. A number of studies have also examined the relationship between firm size and wages, and here it is well established that smaller firms pay lower wages. Moreover, small firms and new firms are found to employ less skilled workers. Most studies also show that new establishments or firms have lower levels of labour productivity and TFP. Since the existing literature is based on a definition of the entrepreneur as a small firm or a formally new firm, and since our study is based on a definition of the entrepreneur as an organic new firm, it constitutes an important contribution to the literature.

Turning to spin-off entrepreneurs, this specific type of entrepreneurial firm is found to be a particularly successful type in the existing literature. Spinoffs, defined in different ways, have in numerous studies been shown to be successful in terms of survival, profitability, and innovation. There are a few papers related to the labour market, that study spinoffs' employment creation. According to these papers, it is unclear whether prior industry experience is important for firm size or not. However, the characteristics of jobs in spinoff firms as compared to jobs in non-spinoff entrepreneurial firms have not yet been studied in the literature. Our study of this issue is therefore an important contribution to the literature.

3. The three papers

The output of the project consists of three papers. In this section, we briefly describe the papers.

In the first paper of the project entitled "Job Creation and Job Types – New Evidence from Danish Entrepreneurs", we extend earlier analyses of the job creation of start-ups vs. established firms by taking into consideration the educational content of the jobs created and destroyed. We define education-specific measures of job creation and job destruction at the firm level, and we use these to construct a measure of "surplus job creation" defined as jobs created on top of any simultaneous destruction of similar jobs in incumbent firms in the same region and industry. Using Danish employer-employee data from 2002-7, which identify the start-ups and which cover almost the entire private sector, these measures allow us to provide a more nuanced assessment of the role of entrepreneurial firms in the job-creation process than previous studies. Our findings show that while start-ups are responsible for the entire net job creation, incumbents account for more than a third of net job creation within high skilled jobs. Moreover, start-ups "only" create around half of the "surplus" jobs, and even less of the high-skilled surplus jobs. In other words, job creation also takes place in established firms especially when it comes to high-skilled jobs. Finally, our approach allows us to characterize and identify differences across industries, educational groups and regions.

In the second paper of the project entitled "Entrepreneurs versus Incumbents: Who Create the Better Jobs?" we turn to an investigation of jobs in entrepreneurial firms and compare them to those in incumbent firms. Even though this issue has been addressed by many researchers before us, we provide new evidence to the field, since we measure the entrepreneur as the organic new firm. Moreover, we distinguish entrepreneurial firms by different types of entrepreneurial firms, and we distinguish between growing and declining industry-region clusters. Our results also differ from the findings in the existing literature. Specifically, we find that compared to incumbents, entrepreneurial firms have higher TFP, are more skill intensive, and pay higher wages. The differences are also more pronounced in growing clusters. However, the wage and skill premiums at the firm level disappear at the job level, as larger incumbents are both more skill intensive and pay higher wages than smaller incumbents.

Finally, in the paper "Job Quality by Entrepreneurial Spinoffs" we investigate whether the quality of jobs in spinoff entrepreneurs is higher than for other entrepreneurs. We distinguish spinoff firms by different types and distinguish between growing and declining industry-region clusters. We find that spinoffs on average pay higher wages, are more skill intensive, have higher sales per worker and are more productive than non-spinoff entrepreneurial firms. The differences are more pronounced in growing clusters. The results even hold when we control for worker heterogeneity and industry and region clusters characteristics.

4. Qualifications

There are two important qualifications of the project that readers have to take into account. As mentioned, we are able to measure the entrepreneur as the organic new firm. In the literature, the majority of studies have focused on entrepreneurs as measured by small or formally new firms.

Statistics Denmark has undertaken extensive efforts to identify the organic new firms. Many of the formally new firms may thus be the result of restructurings or the result of organizing existing or additional activities in formally new enterprises. As a consequence, an organic new firm must not only be newly registered for VAT at the business authorities, it is also required that the firm has not existed previously under a different name/company, with a different owner, or in another legal form (sole proprietorship, partnership, corporation, etc.). Furthermore, sole proprietorships held by an individual who has already registered for taxable activities are excluded.[1] Finally, the data are cleaned for registrations that are due to re-starts of businesses after closure or changes in the firm-registration information. Thus, the set of start-ups used in this project is more likely to reflect the organic entrepreneurial start-ups than if we had just used all new establishments or all new firms, as has been common practice in the literature.

To give an impression of the importance of using the applied measure of organic new firms as opposed to small firms or all new firms, Table 1 presents the number of the different types of firms in the dataset in 2010, where the total number of firms are 188,044 firms.

[Table 1 around here]

It is seen that there are 79,712 organic new firms in 2010. This is the number of entrepreneurial firms applied in the second paper of the project. If we had applied a definition using small firms with 10 employees or less (including the owner) instead, there would have been 165,721 "entrepreneurial" firms; more than twice the number of organic new firms. Moreover, it is seen that some organic new firms are not small, as they have grown larger than 10 employees. This is evident from the entry showing that only 75,215 small firms are organic new firms, which implies that 4,497 organic new firms are no longer small firms.

If we had used all young firms as our definition, the number of entrepreneurs would have been around a third more than in the case where only organic new firms are used. This is seen from the fact that

---

[1] We do not know how many new firms were eliminated as a result of this latter restriction, but if some entrepreneurs start multiple sole proprietorships, there is a risk that this restriction may eliminate some observations from the data that might be considered as organic start-ups. On the other hand, it seems reasonable to assume (and require) that entrepreneurs that start multiple ventures, and where the ventures should also be considered as separate firms, will (and must) choose another legal form than sole proprietorship (*e.g.*, a corporation) for the different ventures. At least from a financial perspective, different sole proprietorships held by the same individual will not be independent entities.

there are 105,894 formally new firms implying that 26,182 would be formally new, but not organically new firms.

In sum, by not using the "right" definition of entrepreneurial firms, there is a risk that we will fail to understand the importance of entrepreneurs in job creation by including too many firms as entrepreneurial firms in our analysis. Moreover, there is a risk that the evaluation of job quality in entrepreneurial firms will be estimated incorrectly when based on definitions of entrepreneurial firms as small or young firms. We conclude that the ability to identify organic new firms is of high importance for the present study.

The second qualification is an important difference between the jobs studied in the first paper, and the jobs studied in the two other papers. The analysis of the first paper focuses on job creation, whereas the two other papers focus on the total employment level. As an example, consider a firm that increases the number of employees by 10, resulting in total employment of 100 employees. For this firm, the increase of 10 is what we focus on in the first paper, whereas we focus on the characteristics of the 100 employees in the two other papers. Imagine further that the 10 additional jobs are occupied by high-skilled workers, whereas the 90 initial jobs are occupied by low-skilled workers. Under these circumstances, the job creation is high skilled whereas total employment to a higher extent is low-skilled. This latter difference is exactly what we find if we compare the results of the first paper and the results of the other two papers, which we illustrate next.

Figure 1 presents the numbers for job creation and total employment.

[Figure 1 around here]

The left-hand-side figure presents the share of jobs with different educational attainment in surplus job creation. The blue bars are for incumbent firms, whereas the orange bars are for start-ups. It is seen that the skill-content of the incumbent firms' surplus job creation is *higher* than for start-ups. E.g., more than a third (33.5 percent) of surplus jobs created by incumbents is within further education; the corresponding share for start-ups is one fourth (24.4 percent). In this sense, incumbents create more high-skilled surplus jobs. On the other hand, the right-hand-side figure shows that the skill-content of total employment is (somewhat) *lower* for incumbents compared to the employment of start-ups. In the figure, it is seen that the shares of employment with medium and long further education are higher for start-ups than for incumbents; and that incumbents have higher shares of jobs with primary schooling and vocational education only.

In sum, we find different results about skill-content for job creation and for total employment. There is nothing surprising about this, but it should be kept in mind when considering and interpreting the results of this project.

References

Birch, D. (1981): "Who Creates Jobs?", *The Public Interest*, 65, 3-14.

Birch, D. (1987): *Job Creation in America*. New York and London: The Free Press.

Davis, S.J., & Haltiwanger, J. (1992): "Gross job creation, gross job destruction and employment reallocation", *Quarterly Journal of Economics*, 107, 819-863.

Davis, S.J., Haltiwanger, J., & Schuh, S. (1996a). *Job Creation and Destruction*. Cambridge, MA: MIT Press.

Schumpeter, J. A. (1934). *The Theory of Economic Development*. Cambridge, Mass.: Harvard University Press.

Schumpeter, J. A. (1943). *Capitalism, Socialism and Democracy*. New York: Harper.

TABLE 1: Number of firms after definition of entrepreneur, 2010

Organic new firms	79,712
Small Firms	165,721
Young Firms	105,894
Small and organic firms	75,215
Young and organic firms	79,712
Total number of firms	188,044

Notes: Organic new firms: Defined as in text; Small firms: Firms with 10 or fewer employees; and Young firms: 10 years or younger.

FIGURE 1: Share of jobs after education groups (Left: surplus job creation; Right: total employment)

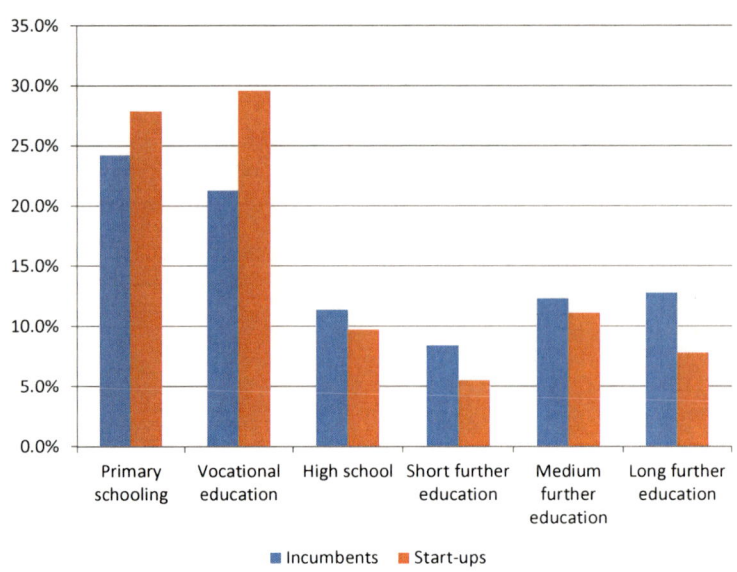

FIGURE 1: Share of jobs after education groups (Left: surplus job creation; Right: total employment)

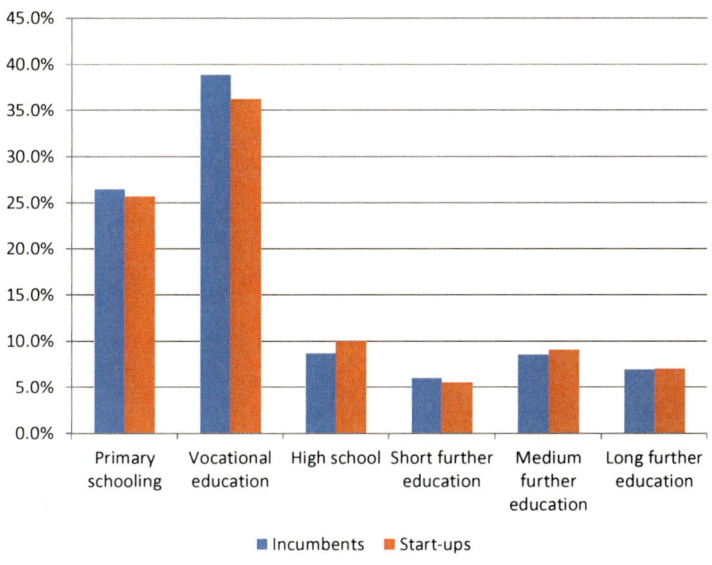